Funny Thing Is

A Guide to Understanding Comedy

Stephen Evans

Abandon hope, all ye who enter here.

Dante Alighieri

The Divine Comedy

Funny Thing Is/ Stephen Evans —
Second Edition

ISBN: 978-1-953725-47-9

Contents

How to be a Philosopher

Metaphysics is said to have gotten its name because it was the chapter after Physics in the Aristotelian textbook. In the classical viewpoint, the distinction between philosophy and science was not so clear as we try to make it today. People just tried to think their way to the truth.

These days, the growth of knowledge is so extraordinary that one person, or even one university, can hardly keep up. Even one area of knowledge can split into thousands of specializations (and more with every doctoral dissertation).

So how can a person be a philosopher today? In the era of specialization, the philosopher must be the generalist, crossing all disciplines to coordinate and synthesize the specialized knowledge, using both analysis and imagination to create something approaching understanding. If language must be created to support that understanding, it is the philosopher's job to apply the language both consistently and critically.

That is the approach I am taking with this book. I am a philosopher, not a scientist. I am proposing, suggesting, elucidating, not proving. That's one of the good things about being a philosopher. Internal consistency of thought and external consistency with evidence are all that are required. Or you can think of me as a theoretical comedian.

This book proposes a philosophy of comedy. We'll examine various categories of knowledge, view the phenomenon of comedy from different angles, put all those viewpoints together, and try to see not just what comedy is, but also what it can be.

Seriously.

CHAPTER ONE

What's So Funny?

Most of what I write is comedy. It feels natural to me. But I also wonder a lot about comedy:

What is comedy?

Is it different from humor?

Why do we laugh?

What happens when we do?

What is funny?

What is funnier?

This book will present my answers to these questions. So it's probably going to be short.

Other people have also asked these questions, really smart people in general. They are not funny in general, in print at least (though some of them do tell some pretty good jokes). But some of the most influential thinkers in Western civilization have tried to explain what comedy is and how it works. In my view, they have not been overly successful, which may explain why Western civilization in general is not that funny.

Although this book is about comedy, it's not going to be very funny either. We'll use the thoughts of these really smart not so funny thinkers to shape our own discussion of comedy.

The Riddle of Comedy

As I said, some really smart people have written about comedy. I'm thinking, in particular, about Plato, Aristotle, Immanuel Kant, Sigmund Freud, and Henri Bergson.

These great minds of Western Civilization have provided definitive answers for the riddle of comedy. Yet all of their answers are different.

Why is this? Well, for one, all of their answers to pretty much everything are different. But there is another likely reason for the differences—comedy has evolved.

Consider the following timeline:

Socrates	*470 – 399 BC*
Aristophanes	*446 – c. 386 BC*
Plato	*428 – 348 BC*
Aristotle	*384 – 322 BC*
Menander	*341 – 290 BC*
Plautus	*254 – 184 BC*
(The Unfunny Ages)	
Dante	*1265 – 1321*
Cervantes	*1547 - 1616*
Shakespeare	*1564 – 1616*
Moliere	*1622–1673*
William Wycherley	*1640 –1715*
Laurence Sterne	*1713 –1768*
Immanuel Kant	*1724–1804*
Lewis Carroll	*1832 –189*
Mark Twain	*1835–1910*
W S Gilbert	*1836 –1911*
Sigmund Freud	*1856 –1939*
Oscar Wilde	*1854 –1900*
Henri Bergson	*1859 –1941*
Will Rogers	*1879 –1935*
Neil Simon	*1927 – 2018*

The human phenomenon of comedy has changed in keeping with (or maybe faster than) our understanding of the world. Comedy in the time of Plato and Aristotle may well have been much as they described it, and those few works from that time that still exist may lead us to this conclusion.

But by the time Immanuel Kant was writing, he had the benefit of knowing Cervantes and Shakespeare. These two alone are a comic revolution.

Freud and Bergson also had uniquely hilarious contemporaries. Lewis Carroll, Mark Twain, W. S. Gilbert, and Oscar Wilde are all deeply funny and fascinatingly different.

(If you want to read more about how comedy has changed over the centuries, I suggest reading *The Death of Comedy* by Erich Segal.)

Can we blame these thinkers for having different understandings of comedy when comedy itself was so different for each of them? Of course not. We should really be surprised if they had not.

(Philosophers can talk like this, making categorical statements to buttress fuzzy conclusions; it is one reason I like being a philosopher).

But there is more to the evolutionary view of comedy. Comedy has certainly evolved a great deal over the last two plus millennia. But the elements of comedy have been evolving far longer, since the beginning of the species itself, or longer. And those elements have evolved independently, on different paths, for different reasons.

To truly understand comedy, we need to understand what those elements are, how they evolved, and how the elements interact to create the unified human phenomenon of comedy.

The Elements of Comedy

The problem with breaking something apart to understand it is that you break the thing you are trying to understand. But comedy is so complex, we need to start somewhere.

So to understand comedy as it exists now, let's look at four primary elements:

- Physiological

- Cognitive

- Psychological

- Semantic

These elements are ways of looking at comedy, and they correspond to particular components of the phenomenon.

- Physiological (Laughter)

- Cognitive (Funny)

- Psychological (Humor)

- Semantic (Comic)

Or, to put it slightly differently:

- Laughter is a physiological process.

- Funny is a cognitive process.

- Humor is a psychological process.

- Comic is a semantic process.

Comedy is all of the above.

These are my terms. You can mix and match differently if you like, but for consistency I'll stick with these.

The important thing to understand is that these components of comedy and the underlying elements didn't all arrive on the human scene at once. In fact, thousands, hundreds of thousands, even millions of years may separate the beginning state from the current state.

So though comedy has evolved (and rapidly) in the last two thousand years, the underlying mechanisms of comedy have evolved over a much longer time. The primary elements of comedy had in the beginning little to do with the phenomenon of comedy, as we know it.

Instead, we can understand comedy as a recent arrival in human evolution that makes use of these underlying states and mechanisms to create its effect. And we make use of comedy according to our own intentions.

Trying to understand the elements all at once is pretty difficult. Most philosophers have generally looked at comedy through the lens of only one its components:

Plato through the physiological

Kant through the cognitive

Freud through the psychological

Aristotle through the semantic

Bergson through the synthetic

(This is a vast oversimplification of all but Plato, but a helpful one.)

If we look at the elements, one by one, and try to analyze them separately, maybe we can at least begin to comprehend the relationships and understand this remarkable human creation known as comedy.

CHAPTER TWO

The Nature of Laughter

Laughter is a survival trait produced by the evolutionary forces of natural selection. And I can almost prove it.

My First Time

I had heard audiences laugh before, of course. Most of my time in the theater was spent as a performer, a singer by choice, an actor (though not much of one) by necessity. But this was different.

In 1980 or thereabouts, I was playing Rosencrantz in Tom Stoppard's *Rosencrantz and Guildenstern are Dead* to small, bewildered houses in a theater outside Washington DC. The play is a sad funny odd take on Hamlet as seen through the eyes of two minor characters, Hamlet's two old pals.

During the run, I got an idea to write a play, a comedy about a playwright inspired by Shakespeare to write a play. I had never written a play before, but I didn't know enough then to let that stop me. I managed over the next year or so to write the first act. But the second act did stop me and I did not finish the play.

Seven or so years later, two of my oldest pals (also veterans of local theater) and I decided over a large Ledo's pizza (the best in DC) to start a theater company. Our first show would be a fund-raiser, a musical review. Our second show would be my play—for which I now had to find a second act.

Production schedules wait for no man, or playwright. With lots of encouragement from my two friends and Shakespeare, I finally managed a second act to my play, now entitled *The Ghost Writer*. As opening night approached, it occurred to me that this was no longer just a personal intellectual challenge— could I write a play? An audience was actually going to answer that question for me.

I think of myself as a playwright who writes books. And I feel differently about publishing and producing. Publishing usually has a wider audience (note the usually), and someone somewhere may let you know what they think. But it is distributed over time.

With a play, at least the first production, you are for better or worse usually right there with the audience. Everything is magnified, and very direct.

The lights went down on the audience, maybe 30 or so, many of them friends. The curtain didn't go up; it went sideways, which was suddenly how I expected the play to go. Then the lights came up onstage.

And sitting in the dark in the back row of the small theater, I was inundated with emotion. But more than anything, more than excited, more than terrified, I felt exposed. My thoughts, my words, my imagination, all were going to be on display.

On opening night, the actress went about her opening business. No one got up and left. So far so good. Then the next actor entered. They exchanged a few lines. And then a miracle occurred.

Someone laughed.

Then more people started to laugh. They started to laugh together (this phenomenon of an audience coalescing to react in unison never ceases to fascinate me; we'll talk about it later on).

There were different kinds of laughter coming from that one small audience. I began to study them. There were the explosive laughs that erupted and subsided quickly, the wave laughs that started small and grew, the quantum laughs that jumped around the audience unpredictably, the lonely laughs from the one person (other than me) who thought it was funny, and the delayed exposure laugh, where it took a couple of beats for the audience to catch up before the laugh.

The audience, that blessed audience, continued laughing throughout the play. Not at the play. At the lines. The ones I had written.

I was hooked. From that moment on I knew that writing funny lines was what I wanted to do. Thoughtful funny lines. Funny lines laden with deep philosophic meaning that would change people's lives.

Or just make them laugh.

That would be more than enough.

That's when I started thinking about how and why people laugh.

Hephaestus Bustling

Since 1927, the following comedies have won the Academy Award for Best Picture.

1934 *It Happened One Night*

1938 *You Can't Take It with You*

1963 *Tom Jones*

1977 *Anne Hall*

1990 *Driving Miss Daisy*

1995 *Forest Gump*

In more than ninety years, only six comedies have won the top award, and none in the last twenty years. Why this disrespect for the art of comedy?

I blame Plato.

In one way, it makes sense that Plato should dominate the Academy. The word Academy comes from ancient Greek. Originally it was a place. Maybe a person too. But definitely a place. And Plato started a sort of school there which took the name the Academy.

Originally the Academy was sort of like a club. A select group gathered, drank wine, and discussed the issues of the day, which in that day happened to be subjects such as Beauty, Love, and the Good. Plato, being the smartest guy in the room, was sort of an intellectual bouncer at these events.

So since they were sitting around drinking wine and talking about Love and such, you would think there would be a lot of laughter. Plato, however, did not approve of laughter. This is odd, because his teacher Socrates was probably a funny guy. Though Plato attributes this opinion of laughter to Socrates himself.

Plato wrote dialogues, plays of a sort intended to be read not performed. The participants were Socrates and whatever sock puppet interlocutors Plato decided to put up against him. As translated, these Socratic opponents sound like an ancient Magic 8 Ball: "Yes, Socrates, it is decidedly so".

But the idea of a group of men (and the occasional woman) sitting around and trying to reason their way to a better life seems quaint and somehow wonderful. We have mostly stopped trying in our time, divided between the Alreadydecideds and the Givenups.

Plato first mentions his concerns about laughter in his most famous work, *The Republic*, which describes his concept of the Just State. Socrates (S for short in the following excerpt) is discussing the qualities of the guardians (the rulers of the Just State) with a young Athenian named Adeimantus (A for short):

S: Neither ought our guardians to be given to laughter. For a fit of laughter which has been indulged to excess almost always produces a violent reaction.

A: So I believe.

S: Then persons of worth, even if only mortal men, must not be represented as overcome by laughter, and still less must such a representation of the gods be allowed.

A: Still less of the gods, as you say.

S: Then we shall not suffer such an expression to be used about the gods as that of Homer when he describes how inextinguishable laughter arose among the blessed gods, when they saw

Hephaestus bustling about the mansion.

Plato again alludes to his opinion on laughter in the dialogue *Philebus*, which is oddly named because the conversation is not with Philebus but a stand-in named Protarchus. But this time, Plato deals with a more general case.

In this dialogue, Socrates is discussing whether pleasure or wisdom is better for mankind:

S: Is not envy an unrighteous pleasure, and also an unrighteous pain?

P: Most true.

S: There is nothing envious or wrong in rejoicing at the misfortunes of enemies?

P: Certainly not.

S: But to feel joy instead of sorrow at the sight of our friends' misfortunes—is not that wrong?

P: Undoubtedly.

S: Did we not say that ignorance was always an evil?

P: True.

S: And the three kinds of vain conceit in our friends which we enumerated—the vain conceit of beauty, of wisdom, and of wealth, are ridiculous if they are weak, and detestable when they are powerful: May we not say, as I was saying before, that our friends who are in this state of mind, when harmless to others, are simply ridiculous?

P: They are ridiculous.

S: And do we not acknowledge this ignorance of theirs to be a misfortune?

P: Certainly.

S: And do we feel pain or pleasure in laughing at it?

P: Clearly we feel pleasure.

S: And was not envy the source of this pleasure which we feel at the misfortunes of friends?

P: Certainly.

S: Then the argument shows that when we laugh at the folly of our friends, pleasure, in mingling with envy, mingles with pain, for envy has been

> acknowledged by us to be mental pain,
> and laughter is pleasant; and so we
> envy and laugh at the same instant.

P: True.

So Plato really seems to have two complaints about laughter.

First, laughter comes from someone laughing at someone else who seems ridiculous. I have to admit, I am not fond of this particular aspect of laughter either but we'll get into that later.

Second, Plato says that laughter produces a violent reaction; that is, laughter can overcome us. He is concerned about this, because he thinks that it will degrade the person, god, or goddess who is overcome. For an idealist, Plato was strangely concerned about image.

For humans, I think what is important is why they laugh, rather than if. If we don't laugh at all, we are in big trouble. As for the gods, if they don't laugh, I don't see how they will ever understand us humans.

What is Laughter?

There is a scene in Robert Heinlein's novel *Stranger in a Strange Land* where the character Michael, a human born and raised on Mars by aliens, tries to laugh. When he can't, he concludes that he is not human. Later in the book, when he has learned to laugh, he believes that he has finally become a true human being.

It's a great hook, but it's not exactly accurate. It's not that Michael can't laugh. It's that nothing makes him laugh. You don't learn to laugh.

Laughter is an involuntary affective non-verbal vocalization. To translate, laughter is a noise without words we make without thinking to communicate how we feel. There are other kinds of these noises: crying, shouting, moaning, and so forth.

Note that there are four parts to this description of laughter:

- Involuntary

- Affective

- Non-verbal

- Vocalization

Let's look at each of those, in reverse order.

Laughter is a vocalization. How do we make the noise known as laughter? In humans, laughter occurs when the diaphragm, the large muscle below the ribcage, suddenly squeezes the lungs, causing air to pass over the vocal cords to make a sound.

Laughter is non-verbal. Though we usually transcribe the sounds of laughter as haha or hoho, these sounds are simply the result of the underlying vocalization, the forcing of air through the vocal cords. We don't say haha when we laugh, we just sound like we do.

Animals, including humans, make sounds for various reasons. Laughter is what is known as an affective vocalization. That is, it indicates mood or emotion. Affective vocalizations are important in social groups that use cooperation to survive. If the guy next to you is holding a club, you'd like to know whether he's in a good mood.

Laughter is also involuntary. When you are an actor, sometimes you have to laugh on cue. It isn't easy. Actually it is so difficult that there are classes devoted to teaching actors the techniques of faking laughter. The primary technique is to think of something funny. Because real laughter is an involuntary reaction.

Some people make a distinction that laughter is not involuntary, but unconscious. There is some truth to this. You can't decide to laugh, but you can decide not to laugh. Sometimes anyway.

There are those instances where you can't stop laughing, even when you want to. I have experienced a number of those on stage, usually when I trip over something. But I have seen it happen even with professional actors on Broadway.

The impulse to laugh can sometimes be irresistible. There was a classic episode of the Mary Tyler Moore show where she gives a eulogy at a funeral, starts to laugh and can't stop. This involuntary nature of laughter happens because the mechanism of laughter is embedded deep in our neurological makeup.

What Happens When We Laugh?

Neurophysiology, the study of the electrical and chemical actions and reactions of the brain, can tell us a great deal about the mechanism of laughter. And gelotologists (scientists who study laughter—I had to look it up) have recently added greatly to our understanding of these processes using techniques such as Functional Magnetic Resonance Imaging (FMRIs).

Laughter is a reaction to stimuli, but that reaction involves different parts of the brain. For example, scientists at the University of Rochester Medical Center have determined that processing a joke or other input involves a part of the brain called the ventromedial frontal lobe, also known as the ventromedial prefrontal cortex. This area is involved in decision-making activities, including evaluating risk.

Interestingly, hearing and reacting to others laugh involves the anterior supplemental motor area of the brain, as well as the nucleus accumbens. The anterior supplemental area is also in the frontal lobe, but associated with different kinds of tasks, such as movement. The nucleus accumbens has a complex role in motivation and pleasure processing (including addiction of all types).

And when we laugh? What happens then?

Obviously, there is the physical act of laughter, which produces the sound. But there are chemical/hormonal reactions as well. Laughter releases beta endorphins, which have a beneficial effect on the body, including stress reduction, pain relief, and increased vascular flow.

Laughter may not be the best medicine, but it is medicine of a sort. There are many survival benefits to laughter. But the most important may be that the laughter response reduces the effects of adrenaline and cortisol, two hormones involved the primitive 'fight or flight' instinct in humans. Later we'll talk about how this fits into a theory of the evolution of laughter.

The World Laughs with You

Someday when you have nothing else to do, go out to the internet and do a search on babies laughing. Today as I write this, there were 2,890,000 results.

Babies can laugh as soon as they are born. They just don't, probably because it takes a few weeks to get over being squeezed through a birth canal. Once they do, sometimes as early as one month old, they start to laugh.

And they never stop. Even Alzheimer patients never forget how to laugh. My father, when he could no longer speak, could and would still laugh.

Laughter is found among all human cultures (except apparently the Republic of Plato). In fact I would say that laughter is what defines humanity, except that in addition to human cultures, laughter or its equivalent is found in all species of primates.

Personally I think other animals laugh too. Birds most likely. Probably whales and dolphins; they are smarter than we are anyway. And squirrels. Definitely squirrels.

But most of the scientific research on laughter has involved primates, so let's concern ourselves primarily with that. We'll save the laughter of squirrels for the sequel.

The social nature of laughter indicates that it likely originated as a signal. But a signal of what?

A Joyful Noise

It isn't only funny things that make us laugh. Any sudden unexpected emotion is likely to do the job, and none more likely than joy. But it must be unexpected, as that crossing of the expectation is the key to invoking the laughter complex.

There is a rose bush behind my house. I cut it back in the spring after the last (I hope frost) and hope the blooms will once more appear. It is important to me, not simply because of the lovely deep red flowers, but also because my father would cut a rose every week off that same bush and set it next to my mother in a small crystal vase.

If I walk out and see the blooms on the rose bush, I may experience the joy of their beauty, and the pleasure of the memories associated with them, but I won't laugh. But if I walk out and discover the first rose has bloomed unexpectedly, I will feel the same joy, the same pleasure, but I will laugh as well.

Does this mean the rose is somehow funny? No, of course not. Laughter is a physiological response unrelated to the emotional experience. It comes only from the surprise.

Then there is tickling.

I'm not ticklish myself. Honest. I'm not. Trust me. A lot of people are ticklish. Just not me.

Tickling produces laughter. Darwin once theorized that this laughter was related to humor, but recent studies have indicated that is not correct. Tickling produces laughter; but it isn't funny.

Evolutionary biologists have developed theories to explain the development of tickling as a form of social bonding, a display of submission to a dominant member of a group, or even a method of communicating vulnerable areas of the body.

Since it doesn't relate to comedy, we won't pursue it. But it provides evidence that that laughter itself was initially unrelated to comedy (or at least served multiple purposes).

My theory is that comedy was grafted onto the laughter reflex later in hominid evolution. But for our purposes it is important to separate out all the other evolutionary uses of laughter.

Why Do We Laugh?

Evolution is tricky because it doesn't start from scratch. We evolve from something to something else. This means that functions get overlaid with other functions, making it difficult to understand how they came about.

Human laughter is like this. While still serving the original primate function of social bonding, at some point it started multi-tasking.

There isn't any archeological record of laughter, no cave drawings of two guys having a guffaw (not that we recognize anyway). So the following is a theory, one that seems plausible to me, though until we invent time travel I see no way to prove it.

A couple of million years ago, hominids (human ancestors) evolved in Africa. They lived in groups and had larger brains than their primate cousins. Sometime in the next million years or so, probably well before language itself appeared, laughter (or at least the physiological function that has become laughter in today's humans) took on a job.

The original function of laughter was probably the aforementioned social-group evidence of mood we still see in primates today. But somehow laughter became also an involuntary vocal response to surprise. Or perhaps the two evolved separately and merged.

This change had two primary evolutionary benefits. First, the social group was alerted to possible danger. Second, the neurochemical and physiological components of the laughter response helped to balance the fear and allowed for intelligent reaction to the event, rather than simply instinctive fight or flight.

The first benefit, laughter as a social signal, is easy to understand. This was perhaps the first step of the evolution from play signal to surprise signal. Early hominids were pack animals, living in groups for safety against predators. This may also be the origin of the contagious nature of laughter; it explains why, when someone laughs, we have a tendency to join in, even when we don't know what they are laughing at. The evolutionary advantage of the danger signal spreading throughout the social group is easy to understand.

The second element is more complex. Laughter suppresses the emotions, especially fear, allowing for intelligent action. The survival benefit is obvious. We have evolved these (relatively) large brains capable of minute assessment of cause and effect, of evaluating options. Yet our emotional mechanisms are derived from biochemical reactions that are millions of years older. We need something to 'give us pause', and let the brain do its work. Laughter and the accompanying complex reactions perform this function.

Remember the three areas of the brain that are active in laughter: the ventromedial prefrontal cortex, the anterior supplemental motor area of the brain, and the nucleus accumbens. These areas are involved in risk processing, movement, and motivation. Here we have some evidence to support the theory that laughter evolved as a shared warning system.

Laughter freed early man to use the clever and creative brain he had evolved. Man is the animal who laughs because laughter helped him survive.

There is a variation of this theory that I have been pondering: laughter is not a variation of the danger signal, but an evolution of the all-clear signal. Once we realize the possible danger event is over, or possibly was never realized, a signal to suppress the danger response and return to normal hormonal and intellectual activity makes sense.

In either case, laughter (and hence comedy) doesn't as many have suggested depend on the suppression of emotion; the suppression of emotion is instead a product of the laughter response. And an important one.

Smiles of a Summer Night

Sometimes we may find something funny but it will not rise to the level of laughter. We smile, finding pleasure in the experience.

As a playwright, I understand this reaction as the result of something wrong with the line itself. Usually it is because I have not written the line with the correct rhythm, or the actor has added a syllable or pause, or has laughed himself, telegraphing the funny.

Or sometimes it is because the thought is too complex to be funny, with the thinking stepping all over the recognition, or sometimes leaping over it and taking the audience members off on a journey of their own.

A laugh is a social event.

A smile is a private affair.

The unaffected nature of the cognitive reaction is what cues the laughter. We'll take a look at this cognitive reaction next.

STEPHEN EVANS

CHAPTER THREE

Funny Thing Is

Sometimes we laugh.

Sometimes we don't.

Always we laugh in response to something.

Sometimes that something is funny.

But what is funny?

A Bottle of Ale

In another book, I describe Immanuel Kant in this way:

> *Immanuel Kant was the Clark Kent of Philosophy, a mild-mannered professor whose super-powered alter ego took the form of an arcane work called the Critique of Pure Reason. Kant's revolutionary intuition was that the mind actively organizes the information it gets from the senses, using categories such as time and space and causation to "make sense" of the raw sensory*

data. Kant's radical principles shook the twin pillars of royalty and religion in Europe.

The Critique of Pure Reason was Kant's revolutionary manifesto, and the primary reason for his fame. But his extraordinary mind ranged further than the a priori structures of consciousness. He also wrote the *Critique of Practical Reason*, a *Critique of Judgement*, and my favorite (not least because it is the shortest) *Prolegomena to Any Future Metaphysics*.

It is in the *Critique of Judgement*, oddly enough, that we find the beginnings of a modern theory of comedy. The following excerpt is a bit long, but there are a couple of decent jokes to keep you going.

Something absurd (something in which, therefore, the understanding can of itself find no delight) must be present in whatever is to raise a hearty convulsive laugh. Laughter is an affect arising from a strained expectation being suddenly reduced to nothing. This very reduction, at which certainly understanding cannot rejoice, is still indirectly a source of very lively enjoyment for a moment. Its cause must consequently lie in the influence of the representation upon the body and the reciprocal effect of this upon the mind... This, moreover, cannot depend upon the representation being objectively an object of gratification (for how can we derive gratification from a disappointment?) but must rest solely upon the fact that the reduction is a mere play of representations, and, as such, produces an equilibrium of the vital forces of the body.

Suppose that someone tells the following story: An Indian at an Englishman's table in Surat saw a bottle of ale opened, and all the beer turned into froth and flowing out. The repeated exclamations of the Indian showed his great astonishment. "Well, what is so wonderful in that?" asked the Englishman. "Oh, I'm not surprised myself," said the Indian, "at its getting out, but at how you ever managed to get it all in." At this we laugh, and it gives us hearty pleasure. This is not because we think ourselves, maybe, more quick-witted than this ignorant Indian, or because our understanding here brings to our notice any other ground of delight. It is rather that the bubble of our expectation was extended to the full and suddenly went off into nothing. Or, again, take the case of the heir of a wealthy relative being minded to make preparations for having the funeral obsequies on a most imposing scale, but complaining that things would not go right for him, because (as he said) "the more money I give my mourners to look sad, the more pleased they look."

At this we laugh outright, and the reason lies in the fact that we had an expectation which is suddenly reduced to nothing. We must be careful to observe that the reduction is not one into the positive contrary of an expected object-for that is always something, and may frequently pain us-but must be a reduction to nothing. For where a person arouses great expectation by recounting some tale, and at the close its untruth becomes at once apparent to us, we are displeased at it. So it is, for instance, with the tale of people whose hair from excess of grief is said to have turned white in a single night. On the other hand, if a wag, wishing to cap the story, tells with the utmost circumstantiality of a merchant's grief, who, on his return journey from India to Europe with all his wealth in merchandise, was obliged by stress of storm to throw everything overboard, and grieved to such an extent that in the selfsame night his wig turned grey, we laugh and enjoy the tale. This is because we keep for a time playing on our own mistake about an object otherwise indifferent to us, or rather on the idea we ourselves were following out, and, beating it to and fro, just as if it were a ball eluding our grasp, when all we intend to do is just to get it into our hands and hold it tight. Here our gratification is not excited by a knave or a fool getting a rebuff: for, even on its own account, the latter tale told with an air of seriousness would of itself be enough to set a whole table into roars of laughter; and the other matter would ordinarily not be worth a moment's thought.

It is observable that in all such cases the joke must have something in it capable of momentarily deceiving us. Hence, when the semblance vanishes into nothing, the mind looks back in order to try it over again, and thus by a rapidly succeeding tension and relaxation it is jerked to and fro and put in oscillation. As the snapping of what was, as it were, tightening up the string takes place suddenly (not by a gradual loosening), the oscillation must bring about a mental movement and a sympathetic internal movement of the body. This continues involuntarily and produces fatigue, but in so doing it also affords recreation (the effects of a motion conducive to health).

Glad you made it through.

There are a number of Kant's ideas that I want to point out:

"an expectation suddenly reduced to nothing"

"the joke must be capable of deceiving"

"an equilibrium of the vital forces of the body"

"Its cause must consequently lie in the influence of the representation upon the body and the reciprocal effect of this upon the mind"

For Kant, comedy is understood as a cognitive process, not a literary product. His understanding of that mental process paved the way for later theories of comedy.

What is Funny?

In Neil Simon's play *The Sunshine Boys*, Willy Clark, an old comedian, explains that words with a K are funny. Pickle is funny. Cucumber is funny. Ls are not funny. Ms are not funny. Tomato is not funny (unless it hits someone in the face).

Willy Clark and Neil Simon are right.

But why?

The word *funny* is a derivation of *fun*, which arrived relatively late in the English language–sometime in the Seventeenth century. Originally the word fun was a verb: to fun meant to cheat or perpetrate a hoax, possibly a variant of the Middle English word *Fonnen*. By the Eighteenth century, fun began to take on some of its modern connotations of amusing, and by the nineteenth century both fun and funny had become descriptive of comic events.

Isn't it odd thought that something so prevalent in our current society would not have a word only a few centuries ago? Then again most of the words related to comedy began to form around that time, with the exception of the word comedy itself, which comes from the ancient Greek.

Funny How

In the human elbow, there is large nerve called the Ulnar nerve that runs in a valley at the end of the upper arm bone (aka the humerus). If you bump your elbow just so, the nerve gets compressed and your arm and fingers go all numb and tingly. And if you are like me, when you do it, you laugh. This area is known colloquially as the Funny Bone.

No one knows exactly how this 'bone' got its name. One idea is that the term is a play on humerus/humorous. What is more likely is that feeling numb and tingly is funny, or possibly that watching someone feel numb and tingly is funny. Or both. Because the word funny has two connotations:

- Something that causes laughter.

- Something strange

The two meanings, though they seem separate on the surface, have a common source. Because funny is funny.

Funny, in its primary connotation, means what makes us laugh. So when you ask what is funny, you are asking what makes us laugh. (Again it is telling that the phraseology is 'making someone laugh', as though there is no volition involved; as we saw in the last chapter, laughter is involuntary).

Think back to what Kant said:

"Its (laughter's) cause must consequently lie in the influence of the representation upon the body and the reciprocal effect of this upon the mind"

That is, the recognition of something funny produces the laughter response. The word recognition is important here. Funny is a purely cognitive process. It may or may not involve verbal interpretation, but the cognition is unconscious, or preconscious. This cognitive processing occurs independently of the semantic processing that may go along with the event.

Cognition is the process by which our minds process input. Some might limit that process to sensory input, but let's use a larger context. Think of consciousness as a mixing bowl; cognition is the cook; it decides what goes in, in what order, and in what quantities.

Cognition does not simply react to what is outside us (sensory input). It also reacts to what is in our consciousness. This cognition of our conscious life results in an ongoing feedback loop.

At the cognitive level, Funny is the recognition of a break in expectation. This recognition is in humans a time for heightened alertness and intelligent action. So the surprise engenders the physiological Startle response which prepares us for action, but the cognitive reaction engenders the Laughter complex. This acts as a control over the accompanying psychological state of fear, which allows for intelligent action and alerts our neighbors at the same time.

So how do we kick off this cognitive reaction? How do we find the funny? And how do these methods relate back to our theory that funny is the recognition of a break in expectation?

There are many ways to understand the architecture of funny. But I think we can divide them into two categories: the preconscious and the conscious. The preconscious depends on structures that do not require an intelligent interpretation. Only cognitive processing is required.

Conscious processing is semiotic, requiring the interpretation of signs, usually linguistic. However, we have to remember that even though the interpretation is conscious, once interpreted, the reaction is cognitive, a preconscious recognition of the interpreted structures. How do we know this? Once again, because we don't choose to laugh.

There is a moment in the film *In the Heat of the Night* where I laugh every time. It's when Sydney Poitier says "I'm a police officer". I laugh. I know it's coming. And I laugh anyway. If we laugh because we are surprised, how can this be?

The reason is that the part of my mind that decides whether something is funny is not the part connected to memory. It is in the cognitive processing, the basically algorithmic processing based on structures that predate language, and possibly even memory itself.

This is where the alternative explanation of laughter may run into problems. Because the funny processing occurs in cognition, the brain must make two determinations, not one.

First, it must determine that something is a threat. It must then determine, in milliseconds, that the cognition is not in the category of threat, then initiate the laughter. There is some neurological evidence of this as a two-step process.

Funny is as Funny Does

So what are the structures that do not require intelligent (conscious or linguistic) processing? In general, they belong to three categories:

- Physical Comedy

- Repetition

- Exaggeration

All of these are cognitive pattern analysis processes. In each of these, the preconscious mind recognizes departure from expectation as surprise and initiates the laughter response.

(Physical comedy can be wonderful, and so can physical comedians: Buster Keaton, Harold Lloyd, Charlie Chaplin, Red Skelton, Lucille Ball just to name (1, 2,...) five. But it is not my thing, so I will leave further discussion to others.)

Funny is as Funny Says

Funny is in the architecture; not the meaning, even if the architecture must be interpreted linguistically. For example, the funny aspect of dialogue is not in the meaning of the dialogue much as it is in the structural relationship of the terms. To understand completely this structural relationship, we have to understand the meaning of each term. But the import of the phrase arises from more than a simple interpretive algorithm.

This is why, in writing funny dialogue, structure is so important. In writing a novel, I find that there are several techniques that are helpful in reinforcing the architecture, making the pattern recognition more certain and the laughter more likely. They are:

Don't telegraph the joke.

Put the funny part at the end.

Craft the rhythm of the line to lead to the trigger.

Leave space after the line for the laugh.

Don't telegraph the joke: Comedy results from an expectation in the reader that is suddenly upset. The set-up line, the line (or two or seven) before the laugh needs to create that expectation. But it can't be written in such a way that the joke itself will be obvious. Don't help your reader to the conclusion; just build the bridge for them to get there.

Put the funny part at the end: Don't step on the joke. It is amazing to me how often this happens. The trigger, part of the sentence that initiates the laugh, needs to be the last thing in the line, or as close as possible as you can get it. And don't put - 'he said' after the line or you'll smother the laugh. Unless 'he said' is the funny part, he said.

Craft the rhythm of the line to lead to the trigger: This is where I expend the most time in writing dialogue: making the rhythm of the line point to the trigger. Get out all the extraneous words before the trigger. Velocity is as important in comedy as timing. A slow line lets the reader catch up to the joke, which undercuts the laugh. And delete as many commas as you can without losing the sense of the line. Commas are the enemy of comedy.

Leave space after the line for the laugh: In a play, actors are taught to wait for the laugh. This is a tricky skill—you have to wait just long enough to know that it is coming, but not too long to lose the momentum of the scene. And one of the great misdeeds among actors is stepping on someone else's laugh, guaranteed to make you unpopular with your fellow actors.

In a novel, you don't have actors to create your timing (or not). So you have to do it by yourself. One way is the in-line rhythm discussed already. Another technique is just as important: create space after the trigger to wait for the laugh. Give the reader something unimportant to create the time to process the comedy.

For example, don't reveal that a character is the long-lost child right after a laugh. If you do, you lose either the laugh or the plot point.

So what do you put instead to create the space? I often use simple business for that purpose, rather than long passages of description. This is why my dialogue reads something like a play. It is spacing for the laugh. Plus I hate writing long passages of description.

Most importantly don't put funny lines one after another. Give us a break.

As you can see, all of these techniques relate more to reader processing of the line than they do to content. That is not to say that content is not important, as we'll discuss later, but that the structural aspects of comedy should not be ignored.

In Cognito

There is a kind of comedy that I have to admit I don't understand very well. Sometimes we laugh when we recognize something familiar, that someone does the same things we do, reacts in the same way to the world as we react.

This kind of recognition comedy is a puzzle to me. If comedy is based on surprise, why should something familiar be funny?

Recognition comedy is distinct from observational comedy, which is often used in standup routines. The unique television show Seinfeld was based around it. Observational comedy is clever, funny and revelatory.

But observational comedy is based on pointing out the absurdity of the recognized behavior. This framing of absurdity uses the same underlying cognitive mechanism as other forms of comedy.

For a species that survives by cooperation, it is easy to see a selective value in recognition comedy. It has the effect of bringing the community together, of enhancing the sense of tribal identity.

I can't quite decide if recognition comedy is somehow the same, or if it is a separate mechanism of inducing laughter, one that has evolved in parallel with the comedy I'll talk about in the rest of the book.

If I figure it out, I'll let you know.

If you figure it out, please let me know.

What is Funnier?

The only writing course I ever took was a one-day seminar taught by Danny Simon, a very funny writer who was mostly overshadowed throughout his life by his genius brother Neil.

I took away two comedy precepts from that day. The first I can never reveal (ask me later). The second and most important was: "What's funnier than that?"

Some things are funnier than others. *Blazing Saddles* is funny. *Young Frankenstein* is funnier. *A Day at the Races* is funny. *A Night at the Opera* is funnier.

But what does it mean to be funnier? In terms of an entire work, it means that there are more laughs, or deeper laughs, or longer laughs, or all of the above. But this is not what Simon was referring to. He was implying that there is something more likely to incite (or excite) laughter than something else.

Here's a brief example of the process (struggle) to find what is funnier:

> *Georg Philipp Telemann, an Eighteenth-century composer, was mostly self-taught on the recorder, organ, violin, flute, oboe, double bass, and bass trombone.*

> *Some people have no discrimination.*

> *Georg Philipp Telemann, an Eighteenth-century composer, was mostly self-taught on the recorder, organ, violin, flute, oboe, double bass, and bass trombone.*

Some people are so fickle.

Georg Philipp Telemann, an Eighteenth-century composer, was mostly self-taught on the recorder, organ, violin, flute, oboe, double bass, and bass trombone.

I am mostly self-taught on spelling Telemann.

Like Georg Philipp Telemann, an Eighteenth-century composer, I was mostly self-taught on the recorder, organ, violin, flute, oboe, double bass, and bass trombone.

I can't play all of them equally well.

Okay, hopefully, you see what I'm trying to do here.

(By the way, the space is to give time for the expectation to form in the reader's mind.)

Understanding the nature of why something is funnier is not important at all to deciding that it is funnier. You don't have to understand funny to write it. In fact, it may be better if you don't (sorry, too late for you now). Because the process that recognizes funny is not a conscious process, but a cognitive one.

Funny On Purpose

So we can see that something odd has happened. Human evolution has co-opted something intended for one purpose and built on top of it to create something new.

This evolutionary process is known as exaptation. The principle was originally identified by Charles Darwin, but the term exaptation itself was proposed in 1982 by evolutionary biologists Stephen Jay Gould and Elisabeth Vrba.

The theory (and it is theory, but then what isn't?) goes that as selective pressures change, the functions that have evolved under the old regime may find new purposes in the new. And that these new pressures may alter the evolutionary path of the old function in quite radical ways.

There are many proposed examples of this kind of development. One of the most common is feathers. The theory goes that feathers originally evolved to help regulate heat, and only later became useful for flight and stuffing pillows.

So in our case, early humans, who have inherited this this laughter response mechanism from their hominid ancestors, have since evolved both larger brains and new sensory processing capabilities. Eventually, my theory goes, this combination developed into a new mechanism to evoke, and gain the evolutionary benefits of, the laughter response.

The interesting thing here is that we have jumped systems, for lack of a better word. We have a cognitive adaptation making use of a physiological system. This is an unusual example that maybe you only get with humans. Or maybe not. I don't want to underestimate the dolphins, elephants, and squirrels.

Of course, this is not to say that the cognitive adaptation does not have a physiological base. Surely it does, just as the physiological systems have a molecular base, the molecular systems have a quantum base, which have string base or supersymmetry base or M Theory base or whichever base you prefer–even theological if you like. But all of these are physical systems–cognition to me does not seem to be physical. It is a metasystem.

The essential condition of a metasystem is that it is not reducible to its underlying components. Comedy itself is a metasystem, so our efforts here to explore its parts are probably limited (though that doesn't imply not valuable).

There is a whole area of study of systems like this, called emergent systems or complex adaptive systems. There is a lot of literature on these subjects; if you are curious, you should check it out.

I would make one distinction: emergent systems have properties that cannot be predicted by the underlying components. Metasystems are irreducible to their components. So metasystems are typically emergent, but the reverse may not apply.

We as humans are probably metasystems. By we, I mean our consciousness, our minds. The jury is still out on whether we are reducible to our components. Some would say there is no psychology, only neurobiology. Some would go further than that, saying there is no neurobiology, only physics. I actually think they may be on the right track, and that the only true system is Everything At Once. Everything At Always, the set of Everything At Once, is an object not a system, because a system involves changes of state.

One other aspect to note is that, in my view, this jumping of systems involves a hierarchy, cognition being higher on the functional scale than physiological functionality. This is a purely human bias, I know, as there is no particular reason to assume that one is 'higher' or more important than the other. But I will make this claim anyway, and extend it.

Remember the four elements of comedy we identified earlier? If not, here they are:

- Physiological (Laughter)
- Cognitive (Funny)
- Psychological (Humor)
- Semantic (Comic)

I think that these elements are really metasystems, in the sense used above, and that they are hierarchical. I mean by this that the cognitive exaptation coopts the lower physiological function of laughter. Similarly I will attempt to show that the psychological system coopts the lower cognitive system, and the semantic system coopts the psychological system.

Why did it happen I this way, and in this order? My guess is simple: this is the way the brains of humankind evolved. Again there are certain prejudices in this view, but given what we know from the prehistorical and historical record, it makes sense to me.

This phenomenon of jumping the hierarchy of systems during an adaptation I like to think of as metaptation.

And fortunately for writers like me who enjoy writing funny books, evolution wasn't finished.

CHAPTER FOUR

Humoresque

So maybe a quarter of a million years ago, something akin to human consciousness began to develop. Archeological evidence shows that representational thinking began to emerge in that era: tools became more elaborate, colors and symbolic forms began to proliferate, and some form of language had probably found common usage.

By 100,00 years ago, paleolithic humans had begun to develop rituals, including sacrifice and burial rituals. The earliest forms of art began to appear not long after, starting with geometric petroglyphs and developing into the beautiful figurative paintings of paleolithic animals, and even graffiti-like handprints.

So it is likely that's somewhere in this period our ancestors began to develop what we now think of as a modern psychology, a mysterious realm of both conscious and subconscious emotional motivation. It is in this realm that comedy takes it next jump in form and function.

Out of Der Witz

Freud's viewpoint on comedy was, as you would expect, psychological. Freud's book on of comedy, published in 1905, is called *Der Witz und seine Beziehung zum Unbewußten*. The title is usually now translated into English as *Jokes and their Relation to the Unconscious*. Though the German word *Witz* can be translated as either wit or joke, neither seems quite right to me.

This problem with terms is not simply one of translation. The problem with the terminology of comedy occurs because sometimes we ask one word to do too much, using it to cover topics better understood as distinct. Other times, we don't make consistent distinctions. And sometimes, the right word just doesn't exist.

As a writer I am a devotee of the Humpty Dumpty school of meaning:

> *"When I use a word," Humpty Dumpty said, in rather a scornful tone, "it means just what I choose it to mean—neither more nor less."*

*"The question is," said Alice, "whether you
can make words mean so many different
things."*

*"The question is," said Humpty Dumpty,
"which is to be master—that's all."*

When you are trying to understand
something as complex as comedy, it is helpful
to be precise with your terms, be they verbs or
no. Freud spends many pages making such
distinctions. He has in fact has written one of
the longest and most in-depth examinations of
comedy. If this alone did not demonstrate his
opinion that the subject is important, he leaves
no doubt in the text:

*Is the subject of jokes worth so much trouble?
There can, I think, be no doubt of it. Leaving
on one side the personal motives which make
me wish to gain an insight into the problems
of jokes and which will come to light in the
course of these studies, I can appeal to the
fact that there is an intimate connection
between all mental happenings—a fact which
guarantees that a psychological discovery
even in a remote field will be of an
unpredictable value in other fields. We may
also bear in mind the peculiar and even*

fascinating charm exercised by jokes in our society. A new joke acts almost like an event of universal interest; it is passed from one person to another like the news of the latest victory. Even men of eminence who have thought it worthwhile to tell the story of their origins, of the cities and countries they have visited, and of the important people with whom they have associated, are not ashamed in their autobiographies to report their having heard some excellent joke.

Admittedly, this is a sort of argument by viral media, which in this age elevates comedy to the level of kittens who play the piano. Hopefully we can do better.

Freud's major concern with jokes seems to be understanding the pleasures derived from them. But he makes an important distinction when he recognizes that there are intentions or purposes behind comedy, and that there is a great deal going on in a joke underneath the conscious operation of it.

He also makes the interesting distinction between the one who makes the jokes and the one who listens, taking the joke itself out of the academic or literary and seeing the psychological dimension. For Freud, the purpose of a joke was to create pleasure. And the pleasure of a joke derives from the lifting of an inhibition, in the permitted expression of unconscious desire. This is something on the order of one of my father's sayings: "many a true word is spoken in jest" though my father borrowed it from Chaucer, I imagine, not Freud.

> *But yet I pray thee, be nat wroth for game;*
>
> *A man may seye ful sooth in game and pley*

In this, Freud was correct. In fact, one of the great difficulties in understanding comedy is that it happens fast, seemingly without conscious thought. There are often mere microseconds between recognition and reaction. Comedy is like an iceberg; most of it floats below the water line of consciousness.

And just as Kant connected comedy with meaning, Freud connects it with truth.

Dream Weaver

Freud's book on jokes came out six years after his revolutionary 1899 book *The Interpretation of Dreams,* in which he introduces his theory of the unconscious mind. I think it is fascinating that Freud focused his investigation during this period on both humor and dreams, because I believe both are examples of metaptation.

The unconscious mind is full of stuff: memories, sensations, and emotions filter through each little universe during the waking hours, while dreams and whatnot fill it during sleep. Do we laugh during dreams? Not that I am aware of, though perhaps we dream that we laugh. But dreams lack the clarity, the fine lines and sharp divisions, that are essential to humor.

Yet dreams and jokes (and humor in general) exhibit the same systemic architecture.

Dreams have a physiological basis; they happen mostly during a particular phase of sleep known as REM sleep, which can be identified by definitive eye movements. Dreams also appear to be involved in memory processing, perhaps reinforcing memories in some way. Dream function also has a cognitive layer, in the interpretation of (in this case self-generated) sensory input. And dreams have an emotional layer, for Freud, in their relation to the unconscious mind.

Every Man in his Humour

The word humor originally referred to a fluid (and in that sense is related to the word humid). During the Elizabethan period in England, the terms became associated specifically with bodily fluids. There were four bodily humours—blood, phlegm, choler, and melancholy—which regulated human emotions or moods.

During this period, there was a kind of play in which each character was dominated by a humour. The most famous of these was Ben Jonson's *Every Man in his Humour*, which marked his first major success. The fact that the plays were funny may have connected the word with the experience, adding the sense we give it today.

By Kant's time, humor had achieved its contemporary meaning. Kant, in his Critique of Judgement, says:

> *The humorous manner may also be ranked as a thing which in its enlivening influence is clearly allied to the gratification provoked by laughter. It belongs to originality of mind (des Geistes), though not to the talent for fine art. Humour, in a good sense, means the*

talent for being able to put oneself at will into a certain frame of mind in which everything is estimated on lines that go quite off the beaten track (a topsy-turvy view of things), and yet on lines that follow certain principles, rational in the case of such a mental temperament. A person with whom such variations are not a matter of choice is said to have humours; but if a person can assume them voluntarily and of set purpose (on behalf of a lively presentation drawn from a ludicrous contrast), he and his way of speaking are termed humorous.

Sorry for the long quote again; Kant is a favorite. The shorthand is: humor, for Kant, is a state of mind. He is exactly right. Humor is a psychological phenomenon.

In addition to Freud's Pleasure theory, there are a number of other psychological theories of humor. The relief theory posits that humor produces psychological pleasure because it allows a relief from underlying stresses or anxiety. The incongruity theory states that humor produces positive psychological benefits that derive from solving a problem. The superiority theory is that the psychological pleasure of humor comes from being associated with a group.

The critical point to note in all these is that the psychological benefit of humor is produced after the humor action (the joke). Psychology does not produce humor. In fact, as we have speculated (or I have, I won't blame you), humor suspends emotions to promote intellectual activity.

This suspension, however, is momentary. The mind is released soon after to feel again. How much of this emotional benefit and feeling of well-being is related to activity at the psychological level (if there is any), and how much is the product of the physiological changes produced by the laughter effect? Here's how I think it goes:

Funny> Haha>Think

Notice there is nothing in that process that indicates a psychological component. But in order to think, we need a certain mindset, which we can refer to in psychological terms.

What are the components of that mindset? Let's put it another way. What are psychological counterparts to the physiological changes produced by humor?

Look back at the theories of humor; it turns out they are all correct: Pleasure (suspension of inhibition). Relief from fear (interruption of the fight or flight instinct). Understanding (the feeling of getting it, of cracking the riddle). Play (the convivial social aspects of comedy).

We understand ourselves as psychological entities, so let's explore how comedy works in this sense. And let's see what effect comedy has on the emotions.

Fear is the Mind Killer

The human brain is an excellent example itself of metaptation of a sort, in which more recent evolutionary developments are grafted onto the more primitive systems, the so-called reptile brain and so forth. Human emotional processing appears to be set primarily in some of these more primitive areas, and many animals (I should say many other) appear to experience emotions, and have the same basic hormonal/neurological setup as humans. Given that the emotional system is so ancient, how can we understand humor as a metaptation?

When I take a walk after it rains, I usually take a twig with me. This is because when I find a worm stranded on the sidewalk, I try and rescue it by twigging it into the nearby grass. When I touch the worm with the twig, it curls and otherwise tries to escape, unaware that I am a heroic figure with beneficent intentions.

This defensive curling and wriggling behavior is an example of the Startle Reflex. The Startle reflex is an involuntary defensive reaction taken by animals in response to surprise stimulus. It happens in worms, and it happens in humans. And it happens quickly, in milliseconds.

We humans think of ourselves as a predator species, at the top of the food chain. But our nervous wiring comes from eons ago, when we were the hunted. We gathered in groups because there was safety there. But not enough. The world was fearful. And that fear helped us survive for a long time.

But we evolved and grew more capable as a species. And the fear that helped us survive now held us back. Fear paralyzed the mind. And for a human in the prehistoric world, when the mind was gone, life was soon to follow. The psychological state of fear, which had been so beneficial to our ancestor species for eons (literally), was now a detriment to survival.

But as we have said, evolution doesn't start from nothing—so natural selection did not eliminate fear in humans, it ameliorated it, suffused it in the laughter reaction, allowing our humans brains to think and respond more quickly and creatively. The suppression of fear opens the mind. And as we will see later, it is this psychological shift which the Comic takes advantage of.

Early in the first book of the Dune series, Paul, the hero, undergoes a test to determine if he is human. The test invokes pain, to see whether he can control his fear and make intelligent choices. Fear is the Mind Killer, goes the Bene Gesserit saying. Frank Herbert, the creator of the Dune books, was on to something when he wrote this.

What would life be like without fear? Humor, for a brief second, by using the funny-laughter complex, shows us.

Meaningless Humor

Some things are just funny. They don't tell us anything about the world. They don't move us to any action. They just make us laugh.

The word I use for this kind of event is humor, because it is comedy that doesn't produce benefits beyond the physiological and psychological. The semantic content is limited, an inessential, even unintended component.

Freud makes a similar distinction. He divides jokes into two categories: tendentious (those with intention) and naïve (without intention). Freud puts it this way:

> *If now we survey the course of development of the joke, we may say that from its beginning to its perfecting it remains true to its essential nature. It begins as play, in order to derive pleasure from the free use of words and thoughts. As soon as the strengthening of reasoning puts an end to this play with words as being senseless, and with thoughts as being nonsensical, it changes into a jest, in order that it may retain these sources of pleasure and be able to achieve fresh pleasure from the liberation of nonsense. Next, as a*

> *joke proper, but still a non-tendentious one, it gives its assistance to thoughts and strengthens them against the challenge of critical judgement, a process in which the 'principle of confusion of sources of pleasure' is of use to it. And finally it comes to the help of major purposes which are combating suppression, in order to lift their internal inhibitions by the 'principle of fore-pleasure'. Reason, critical judgement, suppression - these are the forces against which it fights in succession; it holds fast to the original sources of verbal pleasure and, from the stage of the jest onwards, opens new sources of pleasure for itself by lifting inhibitions. The pleasure that it produces, whether it is pleasure in play or pleasure in lifting inhibitions, can invariably be traced back to economy in psychical expenditure, provided that this view does not contradict the essential nature of pleasure and that it proves itself fruitful in other directions.*

Freud then divides the pleasure derived from humor into three levels:

- Play
- Limitation of critical thinking

- Lifting of inhibitions

Maybe it's just me, but these levels bear a striking resemblance to the states we have identified so far belonging to the process of comedy:

- Physiological (Laughter)

- Cognitive (Funny)

- Psychological (Humor)

Humor stops there, unconcerned with meaning, content with laughter and the accompanying physical and psychological benefits. That's a valid choice. Humor is a wonderful experience and the person who can produce this effect in others performs a great service.

I have a deep admiration for the legendary practitioners of humor: Laurel and Hardy, Hope and Crosby, Lewis and Martin, Burns and Allen, the Marx brothers: all marvelous, all adding to human well-being. I love to watch them for the pure joy of it.

In his weird and wonderful story *The Mysterious Stranger*, Mark Twain said:

"Your race, in its poverty, has unquestionably one really effective weapon—laughter. Power,

Money, Persuasion, Supplication, Persecution—these can lift at a colossal humbug,—push it a little—crowd it a little— weaken it a little, century by century: but only Laughter can blow it to rags and atoms at a blast. Against the assault of Laughter nothing can stand."

Why is laughter so powerful? Because it springboards the human mind past fear, through pleasure, into a condition where it is ready to think. In our world of relentless distraction, how rare and valuable is that?

In our regard for humor and its practitioners, we should also understand that there is more to be gained if we choose.

The comic will show us how.

CHAPTER FIVE

The Comic Convention

Humor is funny minus fear.

Comedy is humor plus meaning.

The Comic Choice

Whenever you write something funny, you have a choice. You can be satisfied with being funny. Or you can up your game and use comedy to accomplish. You do this by incorporating meaning into the process, making the humor about something.

This is where the Comic comes into play. Up to this point in our discussion, comedy can be about pretty much anything. As a process, it is semantically neutral. Funny is structural; pretty much any topic can be presented in a way that elicits laughter. In fact, if you try to be funny about subjects that people think are too serious for comedy (a subject we'll discuss later), bad things can happen to your career.

The comic is how we insert meaning (the semantic element) into comedy. The word *semantic* comes from the ancient Greek word (the Greeks had all the best words) *sēmantikós*, which means significant. Semantics, a branch of linguistics, is the study of meaning.

When I say semantic, I intend something a bit different. And intention is the reason. The comic is the insertion of an intended meaning into humor, with the result bringing not just the physiological-psychological benefits, but the intellectual benefit as well: understanding.

Remember our model: The mind recognizes (cognition) the unexpected and triggers (physiological) the laughter complex which calms (psychological) the fear and allows for intelligence to assert itself. So what are we now going to do with that intelligence just waiting to be put to work? In the comic, we are going to fill that intelligence with meaning.

All well and good, you may be thinking (or you may not), but in what sense is this an evolutionary stage of comedy? It is, in this sense: this stage of the evolution of comedy is not possible without the advent of language, and specifically the narrative structures of language (line, character, and story). These structures make it possible to build on the preexisting elements of comedy, using the mechanisms and results, to impart meaning.

No one knows when language developed in human species. We assume that spoken language developed first, and many thousands of years later, written language arrived. The first evidence we have of symbolic language-like markings appears less than 10,000 years ago. The earliest known recorded stories are about half that old. But it is likely that language began to develop almost as soon as self-consciousness.

In the movie *When Harry Met Sally*, Billy Crystal theorizes that hieroglyphics are "a comic strip about a character named Sphinxie". The record of written comedy actually begins in Greece. The first known prize for comedy was given to Chionides at the Great Dionysia of 486 BC, a big party that was the ancient equivalent of the Cannes Film Festival. By the time Aristotle wrote his Poetics (more on that later), most of the comic techniques we use today were already well established.

Semantic Comedy

There are four ways to use language to bring meaning into humor: Line, Attitude, Character, and Story.

Line is pretty simple, and the easiest to use. You just include meaningful content in the humorous statement, making the funny words about something. Once your intention goes beyond making someone laugh, you have entered the realm of the comic.

The next comic technique involves conveying an attitude toward the content you have added. The attitude can be conveyed in explicit or implicit ways, in obvious or subtle ways. For spoken lines you can use body language, or inflection. Attitude is a common technique in political comedy.

In 1917, Henry Watson Fowler published his *Dictionary of Modern English Usage,* a useful book to which I still refer at times. In it, Fowler identified several different types or devices of the comic, most of which are methods of conveying attitude. It is a list worth revisiting:

- Wit

- Satire

- Sarcasm

- Invective

- Irony

- Sardonic

Fowler, in a brilliant bit of analysis, goes on to identify the motive/aim, province, method/means, and audience for each (well worth checking out in the original text).

Each of the devices he outlines uses the injection of attitude into the humor to achieve the comic effect. For most of them, the attitude is negative, from a place of superiority, and I think this negativity negatively impacts the value of the work. (George S. Kaufman supposedly said that "satire is what closes on Saturday night".) Again, I don't underestimate the power of satire or sarcasm or the other devices. I just prefer other alternatives.

Nevertheless, each of these devices is a way of communicating attitude. The communication of attitude is one of the most powerful comic methods, akin to what Twain was referring to in his remark about laughter.

For me, there is something distasteful about it. I much prefer the glorious absurdity of *Monty Python's Flying Circus* to the sharp topicality of *Saturday Night Live.* There is a shallowness about the later that undermines the occasional brilliance of the writing.

In my view, some comics could use an attitude adjustment. It is not that they aren't funny. It is that they are mean funny. They make fun of, when they could have fun with.

This is a personal preference. I don't like being mean. I don't like mean people. But beyond that, there is something important at stake. There is power in comedy, but the values behind that power come from the person creating it. Comedy can be used to divide, or it can be used to join. It can be used to point at or it can be used to pull closer.

Cultural stereotypes are one example of this kind of humor. We come across them every day, some obvious, some so subtle as to be almost undetectable. Blondes are dumb. Irishmen drink. Geniuses are handsome. But this comedy of separation, as I think of it, perpetuates cultural misunderstandings, and these distort our human understanding.

So what then are the other alternatives? One alternative is simple: changing the attitude, taking less of a superior position, and describing the human comedy, as Balzac called it, the characteristics we all share as members of our species.

One way to do this is to use character. Comic characters reveal the world in revealing themselves. Characters can be standalone, or they can be embedded in story.

Probably the two greatest comic characters in Western literature are Quixote and Falstaff. They are intrinsically funny in different ways, and yet tell us so much about ourselves in the process.

(Who would be next in the list of great comic characters I wonder? Puck? Lady Bracknell? Rosalind? Felix Ungar?)

It is so curious to me that these two characters were created at almost the same moment in history. Falstaff appears in three plays by Shakespeare, *Henry IV (Parts 1 and 2)* and *The Merry Wives of Windsor*, all probably written in the late 1590s. *El Ingenioso Hidalgo Don Quijote de la Mancha* by Miguel de Cervantes was published in 1605, with a second part coming out ten years later.

Outwardly so different, these characters tell us so much about who we are (and aren't) as humans by revealing themselves as human. There is a sense in which both of these characters could be viewed as tragic, as both had unhappy endings (as humans, don't we all?).

Why then do we consider them comic characters? Because they are funny, because they exist within a comic narrative structure (or for Henry IV, substructure), because their creators use the elements of comedy to impart meaning, or, in the case of these two comparably incomparable characters, a vision of the world. This is the ultimate comedy.

The Lampooners

In his Renaissance mystery *The Name of the Rose*, Umberto Eco's brilliant detective monk William of Baskerville attempts to find the killer of several clerics who have been poisoned. Baskerville discovers that the monks were poisoned because they read the last remaining copy of Aristotle's treatise on comedy, which had been thought lost for centuries.

Aristotle's treatise on comedy is really the second part of his work called the *Poetics*. The first part of the *Poetics* deals primarily with Tragedy. If the first part of the *Poetics* had been lost instead of the second, comedy might be held in higher esteem today.

Poetics for Aristotle means something more than poetry; it refers to any kind of artistic creation. In fact, the word poetics in Greek means 'maker'. But a maker of what?

Since the objects of imitation are men in action, and these men must be either of a higher or a lower type (for moral character mainly answers to these divisions, goodness and badness being the distinguishing marks of moral differences), it follows that we must represent men either as better than in real life, or as worse, or as they are. It is the same in painting.

Polygnotus depicted men as nobler than they are, Pauson as less noble, Dionysius drew them true to life.

So, for Aristotle, tragedy is about men of high character, and comedy is about men of low character. He continues:

As, in the serious style, Homer is pre-eminent among poets, for he alone combined dramatic form with excellence of imitation, so he too first laid down the main lines of Comedy, by dramatising the ludicrous instead of writing personal satire. His Margites bears the same relation to Comedy that the Iliad and Odyssey do to Tragedy. But when Tragedy and Comedy came to light, the two classes of poets still followed their natural bent: the lampooners became writers of Comedy, and the Epic poets were succeeded by Tragedians, since the drama was a larger and higher form of art.

As I have noted, we have lost Aristotle's supplement to the *Poetics*, in which he explains in detail his theory of comedy. But we do (or may) have something akin to the Cliff Notes for that document.

In the 1600s, a document was discovered with the grand name of *Tractatus Coislinianus*. This work, only a few pages long, is pretty interesting in that it not only provides a general theory of comedy but specifically how the poet invokes laughter.

Like Plato's view of laughter, Aristotle sees comedy as related to and emanating from the ridiculous. Aristotle had plenty of evidence for this viewpoint, since the primary comics of the day were writing satire. The most famous, Aristophanes, a contemporary of Socrates and Plato, was feared for his wit and his ability to make his targets (including Socrates, in *The Clouds*) look ridiculous.

For Aristotle, tragedy was the greater art. As should be obvious by now, I feel differently. What is the difference between tragedy and comedy?

Here is the shorthand:

Tragedy was. Comedy is.

Tragedy affects. Comedy effects.

Tragedy accepts. Comedy excepts.

Let me put it another way:

Tragedy is a pool. Comedy is a path. You can swim in the pool. But you can't get anywhere. You can walk on the path. But you can't linger.

The difference between tragedy and comedy, at the deepest levels, is that tragedy passes through the mind and opens the heart while comedy passes through the heart and opens the mind. An open mind leads to intelligent action. Presumably, this is a good thing.

Stories are complex, and tragedy and comedy are not exclusive structures. Rarely, tragedy can also evoke an intellectual response, after the fact, in awakening a desire to avoid. More frequently, comedy can also evoke an emotional response. That is, comedy bypasses the heart and opens the mind, which opens the heart.

Comedy then can create a path to a more highly integrated human response. So there, Academy of Motion Picture Arts and Sciences.

Okay, so what about tragicomedy? Would that be the best of with worlds, opening the mind and the heart? Tragicomedy usually isn't. Tragicomedy is usually comedy with a bleak message, or tragedy with a few humorous lines. Sometimes more recently it may be a tragic story with comic characters (I have contended elsewhere that Hamlet is a comedy with the wrong ending).

Still, given Aristotle's more or less disparaging view of comedy, why do I include him in a discussion of the comic? Because

Aristotle originated (or at least perpetuated) the discussion of literary structure. And structure is key to the next comic technique: narrative architecture.

Tell Me a Story

Dante, you may have noted, was included in my list earlier of the evolution of comedy. And you may have wondered why.

The Divine Comedy is not funny. At least the translations I have read are not funny. I read it in Italian, though I don't know Italian, because even the sound of Dante's language is exquisite. But I am still working on learning Italian; in Italian maybe it is funny.

Dante's title for his beautiful achievement was simply La Commedia; the Divine part was probably added later by the Marketing department. He called it a comedy because in his view it was structured like one, rising from the Inferno to Paradise, which hardly seemed like a tragedy.

My favorite description of narrative comic structure comes from John Dryden. Dryden (1631 to 1700) was a playwright and poet of the English Restoration who wrote both

Heroic Tragedy and Comedy of Manners, the dominant dramatic styles of the period. In 1668, he was named Poet Laureate of England, with a salary of "an hundred marks to one hundred pounds a year and a tierce of wine".

In that same year, Dryden published an essay in dialogue form entitled *Of Dramatick Poesie*. Arguing the superiority of English drama over French (which was influential during the Restoration), he describes the comic structure passed down from Greek and Roman playwrights:

> *Aristotle indeed divides the integral parts of a Play into four:*

> *First, The Protasis or entrance, which gives light onely to the Characters of the persons, and proceeds very little into any part of the action.*

> *Secondly, The Epitasis, or working up of the Plot where the Play grows warmer: the design or action of it is drawing on, and you see something promising that it will come to pass:*

> *Thirdly, the Catastasis, or Counterturn, which destroys that expectation, imbroyles*

the action in new difficulties, and leaves you far distant from that hope in which it found you, as you may have observ'd in a violent stream resisted by a narrow passage; it runs round to an eddy, and carries back the waters with more swiftness then it brought them on:

Lastly, the Catastrophe, which the Grecians call'd lysis, the French le denouement, and we the discovery or unravelling of the Plot: there you see all things setling again upon their first foundations, and the obstacles which hindred the design or action of the Play once remov'd, it ends with that resemblance of truth and nature, that the audience are satisfied with the conduct of it.

Though Dryden attributed these terms to Aristotle, in fact, this particular description of the classical structure was likely set down in the fourth century AD by Aelius Donatus, a Roman grammarian (and teacher of St. Jerome) who also devised the Ars major and Ars minor of medieval tutelage. Donatus terms had been updated a bit by Dryden's time, but let's stick with Dryden for now.

My novel *The Marriage of True Minds* originally consisted of four chapters named

Protasis, Epistatis, Catastasis, and Catastrophe—until my agent talked me out of it. But sometimes I still use this four-part architecture as a working structure, until the story develops its own organic form. I like it because it helps me shape the story, connects me to the tradition, and gives me the impression that I know what I'm doing.

Though centuries old, this four-phase comic model can still be effective today. For example, *The Odd Couple* by Neil Simon could be described as:

> *Protasis:* Felix moves in with Oscar.
>
> *Epistatis:* Felix drives Oscar nuts.
>
> *Catastasis:* Felix walks out on Oscar.
>
> *Catastrophe:* Felix and Oscar reconcile.

In my own terms, I think of the four-phase comic structure in the following way:

> *Protasis:* Setup
>
> *Epistatis:* Complication
>
> *Catastasis:* Reversal
>
> *Catastrophe:* Resolution

The term *Protasis* can also refer to the dependent clause of a conditional sentence, the If clause in an 'If—Then' construction. So the Setup phase is the If clause of your comedy, where the general comic situation is established.

For example, in the film comedy *Tootsie*, written (presumably not all at once) by the renowned comic quintet of Larry Gelbart, Barry Levinson, Elaine May, Don McGuire, and Murray Schisgal, the Setup occurs when frustrated actor Dustin Hoffman gets a TV role playing a woman.

The term *Epitasis* may derive from a Greek word meaning stretching, and the Complication phase involves the stretching of the protagonist's dilemma. In this phase, the audience develops an expectation of the comic resolution.

In *Tootsie*, for example, Hoffman falls in love with Jessica Lange, who thinks he is a woman. The comic expectation, the resolution that audience hopes for, is that of romantic comedy: two characters find love together in the end.

The *Catastasis*, or Reversal, is where the hopes of the audience are undermined by interior or exterior forces, or both. In *Tootsie*, multiple forces come into play. Hoffman's character Dorothy has her contract extended, two men fall in love with her, Jessica Lange thinks he's a lesbian, and Teri Garr thinks he's gay.

The *Catastrophe*, or Resolution, is where the complications dissolve and the audience expectations are fulfilled. In classical comedy, this catastrophe (or overturning) meant marriage, the symbolic restoration of the golden age, or the triumph of youth. (Marriage as catastrophe—hmmmm).

In modern comedy, the catastrophe can mean pretty much any resolution, or even just the continuation of hope ("Monsieur Godot won't come this evening but surely tomorrow"). In *Tootsie*, we are given hope of comic resolution when Jessica Lange asks to borrow one of Hoffman's dresses.

But, you might argue, this overall narrative structure works for both tragedy and comedy. And you would be right. Just as the underlying structures of comedy can support both positive and negative comic effects, so also this narrative structure supports both narrative types.

So what is it about the structure that makes it comic? The intent of the artist is key.

The artist who primarily wishes to communicate ideas will find them limited in the Tragic. The artist who primarily wishes to communicate feelings will find them limited in the Comic. This is not an either/or situation. The landscape between tragedy and comedy is a gradient.

For 2500 years, the finest comic writers in the western world have used this architecture to tell powerful stories. How we should use this power we'll look at next.

STEPHEN EVANS

CHAPTER SIX

The Evolution of Comedy

Comedy is sort of a Rube Goldberg phenomenon—the Funny provokes Laughter which invokes Humor so the Comic can fill the mind, creating Comedy. Put more simply, comedy is the tap on the shoulder that makes you look.

Imagine the complexity of the process that developed comedy, in which these four systems jumped one to the next. We have gone from exaptation to metaptation to complex metaptation, or cometaptation. It may be that there are similarly complex human phenomena, but I can't think of any.

A Logic of its Own

In more than two thousand years after Aristotle, no philosopher had written an entire book on comedy. Then Henri Bergson came along.

Bergson was everything a Nineteenth Century philosopher should be. So it is possibly unfortunate that he published his major works after 1900, by which time philosophy was making the misguided Russell-Wittgenstein-induced shift to analytical preoccupations, from which it has yet to be fully rescued.

It was just in the year 1900 that Bergson published his work on comedy entitled *Laughter: an Essay on the Meaning of the Comic.* This is a revelatory title, because it relates laughter to meaning. The relationship of laughter to meaning is of critical importance to understanding both the nature, and the possibilities, of the form.

Bergson understood the difficult task he had set for himself:

What does laughter mean? What is the basal element in the laughable? What common ground can we find between the grimace of a merry-andrew, a play upon words, an equivocal situation in a burlesque and a scene of high comedy? What method of distillation will yield us invariably the same essence from which so many different products borrow either their obtrusive odour or their delicate perfume? The greatest of thinkers, from Aristotle downwards, have tackled this little problem, which has a knack of baffling every effort, of slipping away and escaping only to bob up again, a pert challenge flung at philosophic speculation. Our excuse for attacking the problem in our turn must lie in the fact that we shall not aim at imprisoning the comic spirit within a definition. We regard it, above all, as a living thing...For the comic spirit has a logic of its own, even in its wildest eccentricities. It has a method in its madness. It dreams, I admit, but it conjures up, in its dreams, visions that are at once accepted and understood by the whole of a social group. Can it then fail to throw light for us on the way that human imagination works, and more particularly social, collective, and popular imagination? Begotten of real life and akin to art, should it not also have something of its own to tell us about art and life?

Yet at the same time Bergson reminds us of the importance of the endeavor:

For the comic spirit has a logic of its own, even in its wildest eccentricities. It has a method in its madness. It dreams, I admit, but it conjures up, in its dreams, visions that are at once accepted and understood by the whole of a social group. Can it then fail to throw light for us on the way that human imagination works, and more particularly social, collective, and popular imagination? Begotten of real life and akin to art, should it not also have something of its own to tell us about art and life?

Bergson's point of view about comedy was rooted in his view of life. His primary work, *Creative Evolution*, was published just a few years after his work on comedy. All life for Bergson was subject to the principles of evolution, by which he meant more than the Darwinian principles of natural selection.

Bergson like Kant introduced several useful ideas. First, he proposed the relationship of comedy to evolution (in the broadest sense–the intuition that comedy is something that evolves). And as we have done, he tried to understand comedy through that lens.

Second, he described the essence of comedy as emotionless. The comic effect, for Bergson, was brought about by what he called the mechanization of human action, essentially the perception of action devoid of emotion. In this, I think he was reaching for the element of the comedy that we have seen, the reduction of fear and other emotions that block the mind from thought and the person from action.

A View from the Bridge

Comedy then is a bridge to understanding. But an understanding of what?

Anything really. But in the highest examples (I'm again thinking Cervantes and Shakespeare and a few others), comedy can present not just a view but a worldview. It should not be surprising then that there is a well-defined vein of comedy in spiritual practices through the world and throughout history.

The tradition of the Trickster God is common to many lands and cultures: Hermes to the Greeks, Loki to the Norse, Eshu in Africa, Tenshu to the Japanese, Kokopelli (who like many tricksters played the flute). The Trickster God is often both man's ally and tormentor, sometimes even the creator of mankind. In some traditions, he is aided by the sacred fool, the jester or clown.

The stories of the Trickster God (or Goddess) are some of the funniest in world mythology. In these tales, the Trickster communicates a vision of a world unpredictable and pitiless but full of both mischief and joy.

Perhaps this is another sense in which Dante's work should rightly be viewed as a comedy. It presents a comprehensive and deliberately detailed vision of the Catholic universe of the time. I have known some really funny priests, but in general I think contemporary religious practices have more or less underestimated comedy as a means of communicating doctrine. You might get a lot more people in church on Sunday. At least the Buddha smiles sometimes.

No Laughing Matter

Sometimes funny people get in trouble by making jokes about subjects that certain people, sometimes most people, feel is inappropriate for comedy. The 9/11 tragedy comes to mind. There were jokes circulating that many people decried as tasteless. The Indonesian Tsunami, the Fukushima nuclear disaster, were considered too tragic to make fun of.

Some comics feel it is their job to cross these lines, and redefine what is appropriate for comedy. Lenny Bruce and George Carlin famously come to mind. And so this line changes all the time both within a culture and from audience to audience.

Some comics end their careers as a result. Al Franken, a very smart and funny person, resigned his Senate position because some old pictures surfaced that he (at one point at least) thought were funny but others thought inappropriate.

So are there subjects too serious for comedy? My answer is no, but mostly because the premise of the question is not correct. People feel subjects are too serious for comedy because comedy at its essence is not serious. This is a fundamental error.

Comedy does not discriminate. The human processes underlying comedy do not have anything to do with the meaning of comedy. So comedy can transmit any kind of message. And because in the psychocognitive neurophysiology (okay I made that up) of comedy, the mind is opened and prepared for action, comedy can be not only serious but an extraordinarily powerful mechanism for shaping the progress of civilization.

Not that this always happens. In fact, it rarely does, for various reasons. For one, the people who practice comedy may not understand the nature of its power. They understand the mechanisms of its operation, better than I do probably. They understand that words with a K are funny; they don't know why, nor do they care. It is enough for them to make people laugh. Or enough for them to make money from making people laugh. Or enough for them to feel good about making people feel good from laughing. Or all of the above.

And you know, I sympathize with this viewpoint. Making people laugh is a wonderful thing and needs no further justification of its existence. I love sitting in the back of a theater listening to people laugh at what I have written.

But that doesn't mean we should ignore the further justifications for comedy. Or ignore the dangers from the suppression of comedy. Authoritarian forms of government fear comedy, and rightly so. Remember what Mark Twain said: "Against the assault of Laughter nothing can stand".

Comedy is an instrument of not just persuasion, not just making people think something, but making them predisposed to act on that thought. An audience laughing is an impromptu community, attuned to listening, understanding, and reacting. What else can create that but comedy? Comedy is an engine of democracy (which is why American politicians monitor late night talk show monologues).

So what about these instances where we feel offended by comedy? I understand these feelings, especially if you have experienced the situation the comedian chooses to discuss. So let me suggest two ways of looking at it. No, three.

First, comedy in general is good. It is beneficial to us individually and to the society in which we live. So, as with speech in general, we want to be very careful about putting limits on those benefits.

Second, not funny to you doesn't mean not funny to everyone (even if you think it should be). Comedy is an uncertain art, and it is hard to know without letting it out there what effect you are going to get. That is why comics try out their material in small clubs first. You just don't know. What William Goldman (a very funny writer) said about film applies to comedy: "Nobody knows anything". Of course, this may leave you wondering why you are reading this book.

Third, and this probably applies to more than comedy, when judging a person (and when you condemn a comic that is what you are doing), consider the intent. If the intent was to injure (as comedy certainly can), then judge appropriately. If the intent was to entertain, or better, enlighten, then maybe keep that in mind.

And possibly this too: For some, comedy is not a job or even a way of life; it is a condition of being. And like most conditions, there is a cost.

True Comedy

In the last section, we discussed the responsibility of the audience. What about the responsibility of the practitioners?

Comedy is like a gun. You can point it in pretty much any direction. That is, the structural effects that generate the cognitive and psychological reaction can be used for most any intended purpose.

So here is my plea to the comedians of the world: Laugh with them, not at them. Don't make fun of. Have fun with.

Comedy has power. We need to temper that power with wisdom. We need to use that power with understanding.

Comedy is an extraordinary accident, a bizarre and unexpected addendum to the human psyche that enriches our lives. A phenomenon that began millions of years ago as primate play has the potential to transform our lives and our civilization.

But how do we realize this potential? How do we make the best use of this extraordinary accident?

The first step of course is to understand that the potential exists. Comedy opens minds. Open minds can change. Comedy has a unique power to alter our understanding of the world we live in, which can alter the world we live in.

The next step is to accept that comedy can have many uses. Some of those uses are beneficial. Some are not. Some are essential to the progress of civilization. I refer to this type as True Comedy.

A pretentious title, you might think. Maybe so. But I don't mean to say that some comedy is true and others false. What I mean is that some comedy, the rarest form unfortunately (maybe we can change that) is comedy that leads us toward truth. True comedy opens the mind and keeps it open.

So the third step is to recognize this form of comedy, value it when we find it, aspire to it, and practice it as best we are able. If you are taking the trouble to open someone's mind, you have an obligation to fill it with something worthwhile.

Truth comes to mind.

Kindly Create

In the movie version of Harvey, the character of Elwood P. Dowd says, "Years ago my mother used to say to me... She'd say, 'In this world, Elwood, you must be'—she always called me Elwood—'in this world, Elwood, you must be oh so smart or oh so pleasant.' Well, for years I was smart. I recommend pleasant. You may quote me."

I do, obviously. It is one of my favorite lines in one of my favorite films. I don't see six-foot-tall rabbits (or none I'm admitting to). But sometimes I think that something like his transformation may have happened to me. For years, I was smart, but being smart didn't make me a writer.

Twenty years ago, I decided I was supposed to be a writer. I thought about writing. I read books about writing. But I wasn't actually doing any writing.

So, feeling the years slipping by, I quit my job and headed out across the country, intending to write a book. Yet mile after mile, I wrote nothing, except a few emails about amazing scenery and how often I got lost. Eventually, I gave up and turned toward home.

A thousand miles or so later, a butterfly got caught in my windshield wipers. I slowed down and got off the highway at the next opportunity, coaxed the little guy onto a sheet of (blank, no doubt) paper, and set him onto a patch of grass near some woods. He couldn't fly anymore, but he could walk. I watched each slow, painstaking step until he disappeared into the brush. Then I got back in my car and on the highway.

Moments later, a poem came to me about the butterfly. Quickly, I dictated the words into my recorder. It wasn't great poetry. But it was the first creative writing I had done in a long time.

That night, I sat at a desk in my hotel room and began to write. I didn't stop until I had finished the entire first act of a play, and then, over the next few years, finally a book about that trip called *A Transcendental Journey*.

Since I wrote *A Transcendental Journey*, so much of my life has revolved around taking care of family—a time that has also been the most creative of my life. I think there is a connection.

I began *The Marriage of True Minds*, my first novel, while I was taking care of my aunt Margaret, to whom it is dedicated. I edited the novel while staying with my friend Don in what turned out to be the last months of his life. The final piece of the story was based on the eulogy I wrote for my brother Michael.

A few years later, when both of my parents were diagnosed with health issues, I moved in to take care of them. My writing during those years consisted mostly of short pieces, now collected in *Liebestraum*. I think it is some of my best work.

After my parents passed away, I was lucky to be able to take some time off. I thought I needed it—needed to get back to being the person I used to be. I never did. I don't think now I will. And I wouldn't choose to if I could, as a man or as a writer.

In a year, I wrote drafts of a play and two books, plus half of a third. The play has been produced. The two books have been published. This is the third.

I don't really like the word *caregiving*: it is too one-sided. Caring for someone is a shared experience, often both deeply rewarding and deeply draining. But in each case in my life, I don't doubt that some reflection of that shared experience, and of the person I shared it with, has gone into the work.

As a writer, my instinct is to wrap myself up in a solitary world—to live in the one I am creating. But I have realized that what works for me may be the opposite: turn out, see the world, do what needs to be done for the people in your life. And as you do, trust that the wheels are turning in your imagination.

What does this have to do with comedy? Only this: living kindly, opening up to compassion in your life, connects you to the vital part of yourself that is the engine of creativity. And in turn this compassion will flow through this creativity, shaping the product in profound ways.

Caring is the wildest fuel for the creative fire.

You may quote me.

Let Me Sum Up

So, we have the four primary elements of comedy:

- Physiological
- Cognitive
- Psychological
- Semantic

To which we have attributed the following designations:

- Laughter
- Humor
- The Funny
- The Comic

We have evolved through each stage or system or building block or what have you to arrive over millions of years and who knows how many species at the supremely complex human phenomenon of Comedy.

But as I noted earlier, evolution isn't finished. Which begs the question: what is next? Honestly, I have no idea. It's hard enough to understand the Comedy that exists today.

But I can l tell you what I hope for. I hope for a Comedy Consciousness, a result of all that post-laughter pondering, which will fill the world with its dazzling light of understanding and hope.

We made it to Comedy. Whose says we can't make it the rest of the way?

Not me.

Go Forth in Comedy

I say this unto you: go forth in Comedy.

Go ye among them and contribute to the maturity of our civilization.

Elevate our little planet and the denizens thereof.

Foment laughter.

Ease hearts.

Fill minds.

In this way shall you be numbered among the elect unto the end of days.

And possibly be considered for a Prime Time HBO Special.

Amen.

STEPHEN EVANS

Bibliography

The Republic, Plato, translation Benjamin Jowett

Philebus, Plato, translation Benjamin Jowett

Poetics, Aristotle, translation S. H. Butcher

Tractatus Coislinianus, Unknown

Preface to the Works of John Dryden, Samuel Johnson

Of Dramatick Poesie, An Essay, John Dryden, edited by Jack Lynch

The Critique of Judgement, Immanuel Kant, translation James Creed Meredith

Jokes and their Relation to the Unconscious, Sigmund Freud, translation A. A. Brill

Laughter: An Essay on the Meaning of the Comic, Henri Bergson, translation Cloudesley Brereton and Fred Rothwell

The Death of Comedy, Erich Segal

Henry IV Parts 1 and 2, William Shakespeare

The Merry Wives of Windsor, William Shakespeare

Don Quixote, Miguel de Cervantes

Every Man In His Humor, Ben Jonson

Dictionary of Modern English Usage, Henry Watson Fowler

More Interesting Things to Read

Laughter: A Scientific Investigation (Robert R. Provine)

Laughter: Nature or Culture (Moira Smith, Indiana University)

The expressive pattern of laughter (Ruch, W., & Ekman, P. (2001).

Neural circuit of verbal humor comprehension in schizophrenia - an fMRI study (Przemysław Adamczyk, Miroslaw Wyczesany, Aleksandra Domagalik, Artur Daren, Kamil Cepuch, Piotr Błądziński, Andrzej Cechnicki, and Tadeusz Marek)

Social laughter is correlated with an elevated pain threshold (R. I. M. Dunbar, Rebecca Baron, Anna Frangou, Eiluned Pearce, Edwin J. C. van Leeuwen, Julie Stow, Giselle Partridge, Ian MacDonald, Vincent Barra, and Mark van Vugt)

Marina Davila Ross, Michael J Owren, and Elke Zimmermann)

The Spandrels of San Marco and the Panglossian Paradigm: A Critique of the Adaptationist Programme (Stephen Jay Gould and Richard Lewontin)

Exaptation — a missing term in the science of form (Stephen Jay Gould and Elizabeth Vrba)

The functional anatomy of humor: segregating cognitive and affective components (Vinod Goel and Raymond J. Dolan)

Acknowledgements

In my family, I was the serious one. But I grew up in a family where one of the main ingredients to any meal was laughter.

My father was a wonderful teller of funny stories, my mother a wonderful listener. My three brothers each possessed some variation of the Evans sense of humor. I learned from them, from my very funny friends, from the audiences I performed for, from the actors who performed my work.

Somehow it has all led to this, which I hope will lead to more Comedy in the world. We could use it.

I hope I have done my part.

I hope in your way you will do yours.

STEPHEN EVANS

About the Author

Stephen Evans is a playwright and the author of *A Transcendental Journey, Painting Sunsets,* and *The Island of Always.* Find him online at:

https://www.istephenevans.com/

https://www.facebook.com/iStephenEvans

https://twitter.com/iStephenEvans

S<small>TEPHEN</small> E<small>VANS</small>

Books by Stephen Evans

Fiction:

The Island of Always Series:
    The Marriage of True Minds
    Let Me Count the Ways
    My Winter World
Whose Beauty is Past Change
The Marriage Gift
Paradox
The Mind of a Writer and other Fables
Some Version of This is Funny: Jokes and Observations
The Next Joy and the Next: A Mythology

Non-Fiction:

Prolegomena to Any Future Vacation
Funny Thing Is: A Guide to Understanding Comedy
The Laughing String: Thoughts on Writing
Layers of Life: Essays and Aphorisms
Liebestraum

Plays:

The Visitation Quartet:
    The Ghost Writer
    Monuments
    Tourists
    Spooky Action at a Distance
Experience   (Three One-Act Plays about Ralph Waldo Emerson)
Generations   (with Morey Norkin and Michael Gilles)
As You Like It   (by William Shakespeare, adapted by Stephen Evans)
The Glass Door   (An Adaptation of Hedda Gabler by Henrik Ibsen))

Verse:

Limerosity
Limerositus
Sonets from the Chesapeke
A Look from Winter

STEPHEN EVANS